# FORBIDDEN BUT OH, SO SWEET

LILY LAMKIN

*for baxter*

I am forever grateful for the role you have played in my life. The deep feelings I have felt with you have been a breathtaking addition to my human experience. I could not have transcended to the person I am today without all the pleasure, but especially all the *pain* our relationship has provided.

Thank you, my love.

# TABLE OF CONTENTS.

maybe we are twin flames
maybe we are karmic partners
at this point
i am torn between the two
i don't know now
and i may never know
exactly how to define
our connection
maybe it can't be defined
or shouldn't be
we try to gain
a deeper understanding
in order to cope
but i think i will
just let this one be
what it is
a mystery

- soul tie

i felt drawn to you
since the moment i met you
like a magnetic pull
the closer we got
the more irresistible the union
i didn't care
who i hurt in the process
i craved you
only you

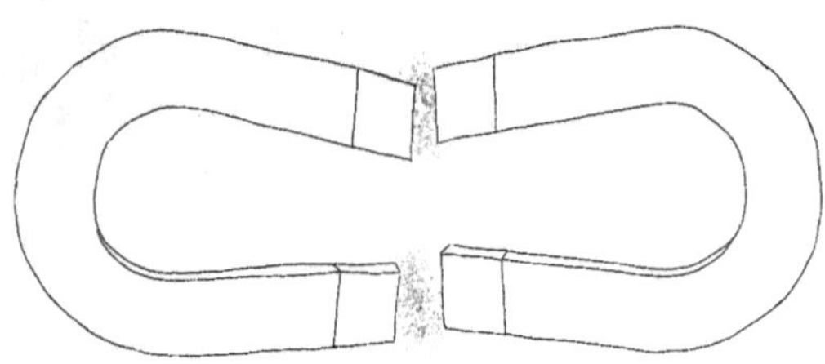

running down the road
in the darkness
i parked my car far away
so your parents didn't know
i was there
bottle of wine in hand
we run as fast as we can
you sneak me in
through your bedroom window
which became a regular occurrence
when we weren't quite done
being with each other
after 10 o'clock
it was the thrill
it made me feel so alive
i wish i could trade
the bruises on my heart
for the bruises
on my thighs
from the window sill

- be back in 5

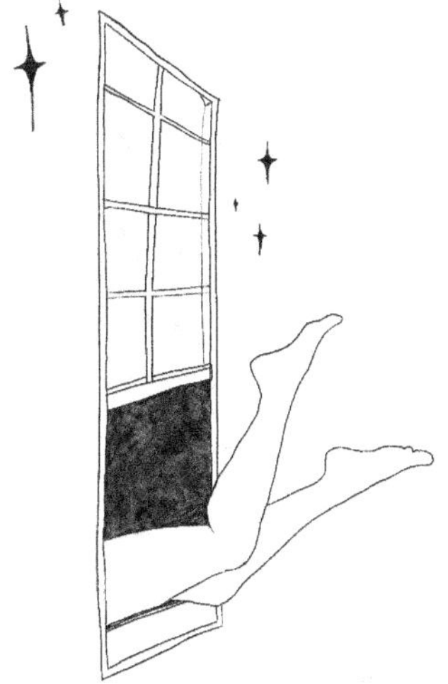

just friends
we were just friends
everyone knew this was a lie
even we knew it
i think we were scared
scared of labeling
this amazing connection
scared of having it
scared of losing it
scared of hurting
everything was perfect
just the way it was
so why be anything more
than just friends

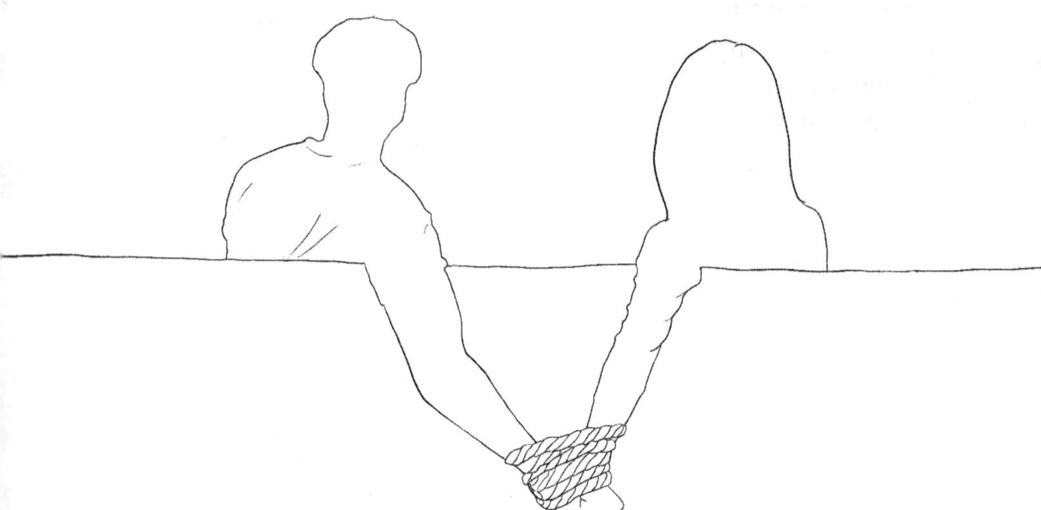

we talked for hours
in the walmart parking lot
late at night
discussed our lives
before each other
our hardships
our acheivements
our hopes
our dreams
our fears
our feelings
you showed me music
music was your favorite
i loved how deeply it touched you
watching the fire in your eyes
you were so excited to share
this special part of your life
with me
i reflect on these early moments often
looking back on them fondly
and that is all they will ever be now
memories

grocery shopping
such a mundane task
but it was one of my favorites
with you
joking around
laughing
teasing each other
always
that's someone
i wanna do life with
that's the thing about you
you bring out the little kid in me
my inner child
she is awakened
with you
in so many ways

- i'll race you down the aisle

nothing warmed my heart more
than the delicious meals
you always made me
you poured so much of your
heart and soul
into your culinary creations
and i could taste it
i could feel it
it was perfect
for the girl
who doesn't feed herself
it was your way
of caring for me
of loving me
if only we could sit down today
and enjoy some yummy tacos
together

- warm comforts

here we go again
escaping reality together
as we do best
puff puff
cough cough
i smoked too much this time
my mind races
my body shakes
i can't breathe
so i breathe
faster
faster
faster
anxiety courses through my veins
i feel it head to toe
what I need right now
dark
quiet
& you

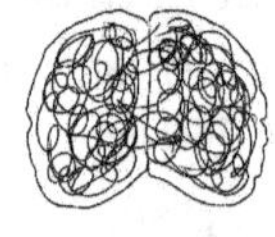

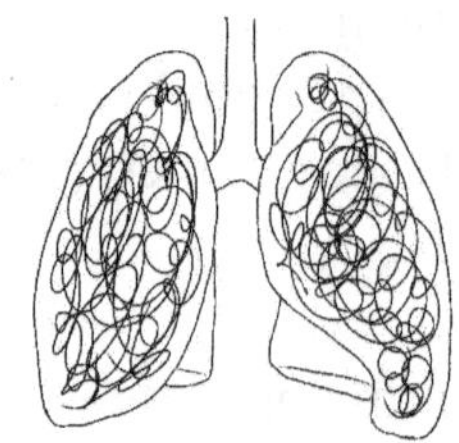

turn the lights off
the music, off
we lay on the bed
i lie on top of you
to be held tightly by you
is all i need now
but your arms touch my back
limp
no embrace
like you don't want me there
so i move over
where i'm not a bother
i try to reach for you again
and you offer what you can
but that isn't much
your energy towards me
so closed off
so i do it myself
i let the panic run it's course
with two thirds of what i needed
dark & quiet
i'll feel better soon
and i'll get there
i always do
with or without you

little gifts
little surprises
were your favorite thing to give
you always thought
you weren't very good
at giving gifts
but i thought otherwise
one day you got me
these little spongebob toys
you knew it had been my favorite
childhood cartoon
you hid them
throughout your house
as i spent the evening
finding them
you see
it wasn't anything big
but it was all of the
little things
that led me to
falling in love with you

- inner child

call me pretty
call me beautiful
flirt with me
please
i beg of you
not because i need
the validation
not because i need
the compliments
because you're giving
that energy
to other girls
and not me
i'm supposed to be
your number one
i find myself green
with envy
of the playful energy
you give to others
that should be me
that should be me

- good morning beautiful

it was impressive
how we could take
one seemingly insignificant topic
and turn it into
a full blown fight
sometimes we yelled
you much more than me
but still
we were experts
at forgetting
that we loved each other
and suddenly we became enemies
saying whatever thought came to mind
no filter
no consideration
for how deeply
words can cut
they cut deep
i still have scars from them
they have healed
but they will never go away
& you can't take those words
back

- sharp words

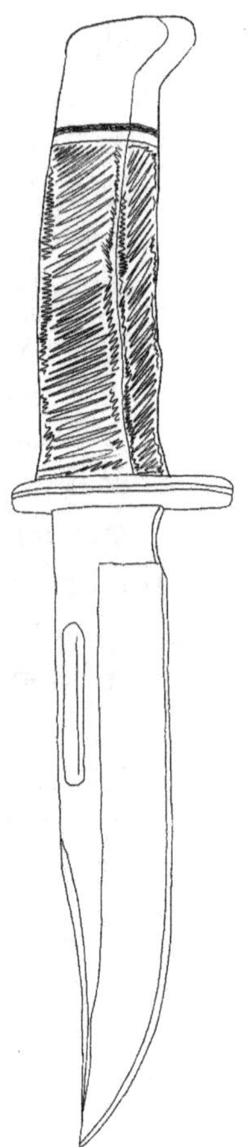

the water runs down my back
the drugs run through my veins
your fingers run through my hair
bliss
our naked bodies
intertwined as one
our souls speak to each other
through our eyes
through our touch
through our embrace
never let me go
i feel undoubtedly safe
i feel passionately loved
my soul is home
please don't let me go

- let's save water

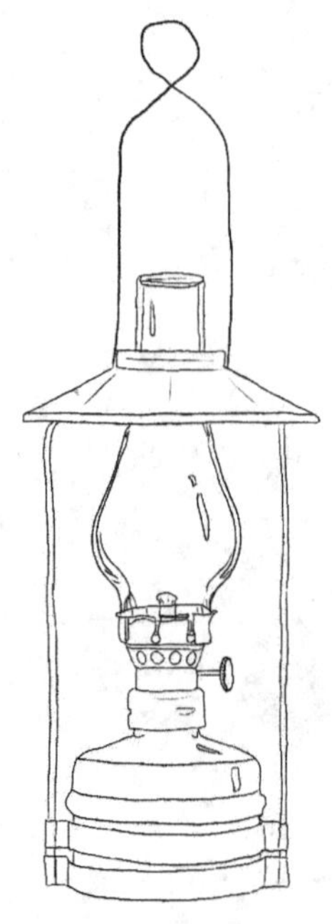

triggers are funny little things
even just one word
my heart begins pound
first i can feel it in my chest
then i can hear it
the tips of my fingers
it's like they aren't there
i cannot feel them anymore
and now i can't feel my hands
the only sensation left
is a tingle
the pins & needles multiply
my lungs cannot find enough air
as they desperately search
they are unsatisfied still
the tears stream down my cheeks
confused
my body is so scared
and my mind doesn't know why

you know how to touch me
like no other has
not even myself
your mouth
your tongue
a portal to pure pleasure
tears stream down my face
i cry
for the feeling is overwhelming
the intensity
like never before
my body twitches
i cannot think
i cannot speak
only feel
feel
feel

touching your skin feels like home
you are home to me
you will always be home to me

- homeless

curls
they melt me
i always wanted
my babies
to have
your curls

"we had our time in the sun"
as you said
those bright, shining, innocent moments
before there was any darkness
to dim the shine we felt
we have stayed too long
we are sunburnt
those words
have brought me to my knees
because right now
there is nothing more beautiful
yet painful
than the intoxicating memories
of our time in the sun

you and i
we exist
in two separate
universes
so far away
so alien
to each other
yet
the link between
our opposing worlds
is strong
and when we exist
within that link
it's nirvana

i suppose nothing that intense
powerful
all-consuming
can last forever
the brighter the star
the faster it dies

i wanted you to change who you are?
no.
i wanted you to grow
i guess i forgot a crucial detail though
that you didn't want to grow with me

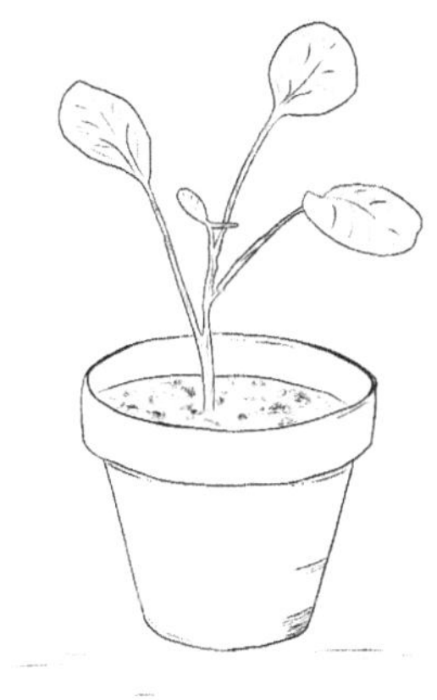

you compare me to your vices
i am the alcohol in your veins
i am the nicotine in your lip
i am the weed filling your lungs
the things you are most drawn to
hurt you
but of all the vices
you quit me cold turkey

- why me

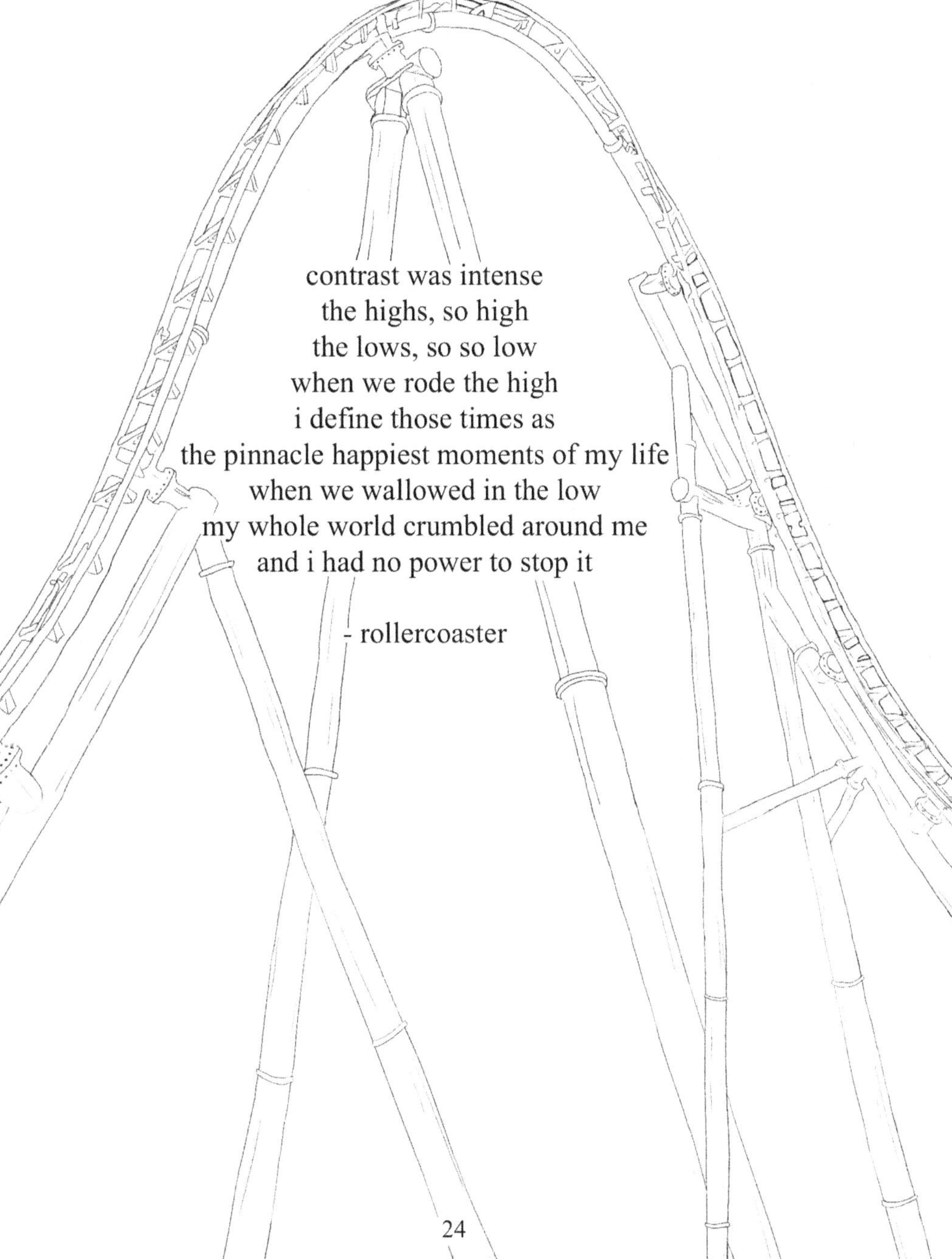

contrast was intense
the highs, so high
the lows, so so low
when we rode the high
i define those times as
the pinnacle happiest moments of my life
when we wallowed in the low
my whole world crumbled around me
and i had no power to stop it

- rollercoaster

she cries
and cries
hoping that he tries
doesn't fill the space with lies
he's not like the other guys
but he fills his cup with highs
leading to his own demise
she asks herself the whys
it only makes her despise
something inside her dies
now she has puffy eyes
but maybe
if he's kisses her thighs
there won't be dark skies
honey, please be wise

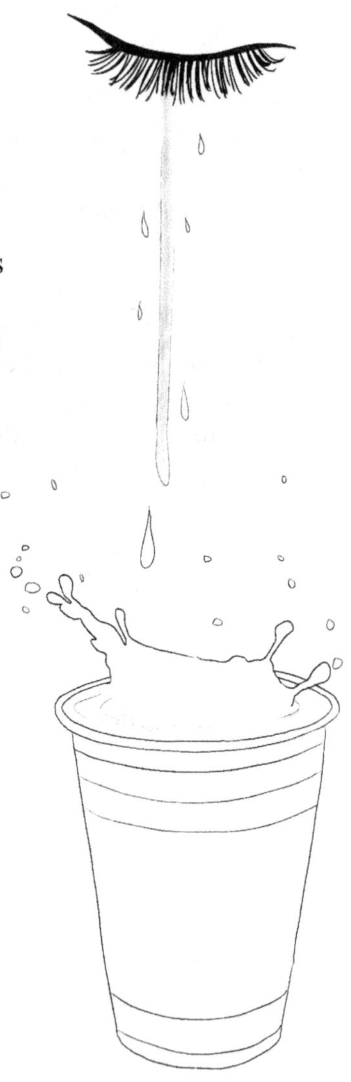

white heat
within one strike of a match
our hearts on fire
our love ablaze
burning brighter
hotter
than i've ever experienced
but we cannot forget
the laws of nature
the hotter a flame burns
the more it requires to stay alive
and therefore the faster the flame
becomes just smoke
black smoke

i wish you
had the capacity
to love me
with the magnitude
to which i
love(d) you

- potential

i left my shoes on
drove into your driveway
with a pit in my stomach
knowing there is no chance
we can save this anymore
yet i still
have this glimmer of hope
that maybe
just maybe
you will hug me and not let go
tell me there is nothing more
you want in this world
than us
than this
but i can see it in your eyes
there is no fight left in you
this is over
and there is nothing left to do
but to leave
a single tear
streams down your face
i stand up
and walk out
i knew this would be our fate
this is why
i left my shoes on

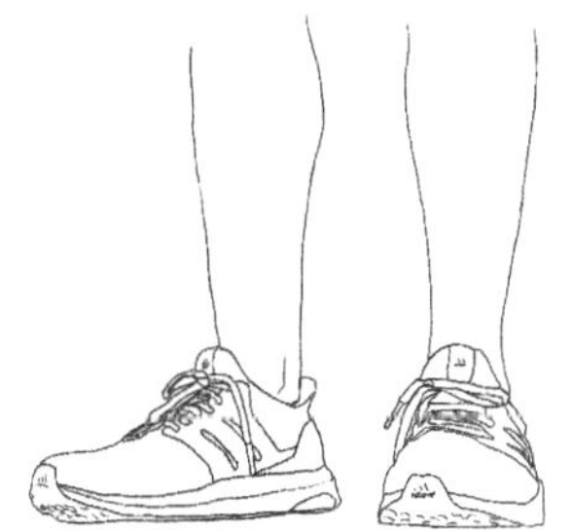

the shower
a place of comfort
the hot water
rains down on your weary skin
wrapping your body
in a warm hug
in the dark clouds of
depression
sitting on the shower floor
is commonplace
but today,
in the shower i scream
yell at the top of my lungs
the pain of knowing it's over
between us
cannot be contained
luckily i'm alone
if anyone was around
they would barge through
the bathroom door
expecting to see
me bleeding on the floor

after our first ending
i was bitter
i was so *so*
bitter
i was angry with you
with how we left things
with how quickly
you seemed to move on
and forget me
which i later came to know
that you never did really
move on
i hate the person
i became then
she was mean
resentful
& oh, goodness
so vengeful
i can find peace in knowing
that i am not her anymore
i have conducted myself
with poise and grace
grieving properly
in a healthy manner
something i had never
really leaned into before
this kind of self-love
i have cultivated
is uncharted territory for me

- overflowing

on the rooftop
we shared the night with the stars
in a haze of smoke
we let our deepest feelings flow
your head in my lap
my tears falling on your face
as natural as the rain on your skin
what if it's you
what if you're the one
what if i have a husband
what if i have children
what if i have the perfect little life
without you
and what if i still can't stop asking myself
what if?

dancing in a drunken sea
people surrounding us
but all i see is you
you hold me close to you
i can feel your spirit
your energy
and in this very moment
it is dancing with mine
i've never felt so close to you
i've never felt so in sync with another soul
than i do right now
if i could live in this moment forever
i would

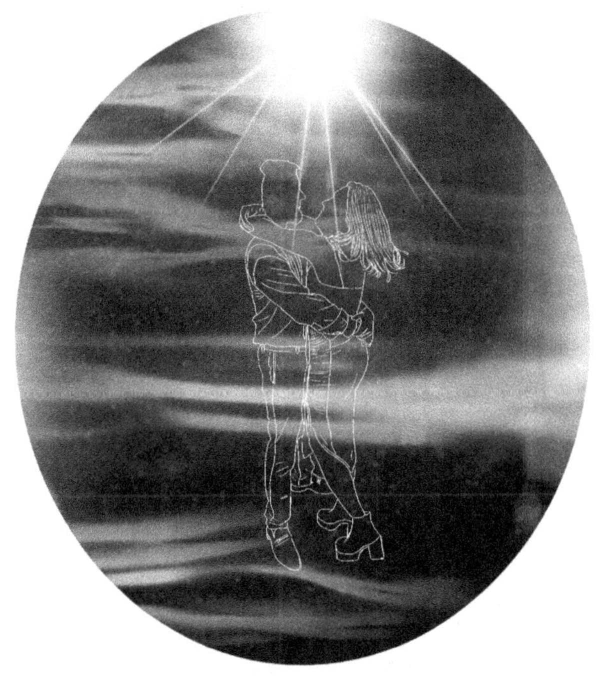

our sex was gifted to us
from the cosmos
with such beautiful intensity
and closeness
it was simply not earth-born
the energy of our souls
making magic
so in sync
so close, almost intertwined
we reach ecstasy
simultaneously
a pinnacle experience
to share with another soul
nothing else in this universe
makes me weaker
i surrender

it's a tragic love story really
two humans
hopelessly in love
so perfectly aligned
yet so horribly crossed
twisted
intertwined
& paradoxically
out of alignment
it makes no sense
yet makes perfect sense
can't exist apart
or together
even though you aren't with me
you will always be with me
whether i want the company
of your soul
or not

- no escape

never did i believe
that i was a fighter
a *physical* fighter
you never really know
how you will react
until faced with the opportunity
so when her fist met your cheek
there was no forethought
no plan
no consideration
of my actions
just an instant reaction
which happened to be violence
you really do blackout in those moments
don't feel any pain
your body just takes over
fists swinging
hair-pulling
biting
dirty, dirty fighting
i was lucky to walk away
with a few scratches
and some missing hair
but i don't know what came over me
my subconscious
chose to defend you
at all costs
no matter what

- primal

i look in the mirror
i see beauty
i see strength
i see confidence
but when i'm with you
when we are deeply intertwined
in each other's lives
that beauty
that strength
that confidence
it begins to fade away
i begin to lose myself
my glow fades
and my cup
fills up
with insecurity

- why do you make me feel this way

never before
have i met a human
who has so much self-love
yet carries
so much self-hate
at the same time

- isn't it heavy?

there is nothing
more heart-wrenching
than watching the smile
the joy
the happiness
slowly drain
out of their face
their eyes
their smile
the glow
it fades
ever so slowly
in the photos
over time
you try to not see it
but it's right there
undeniable

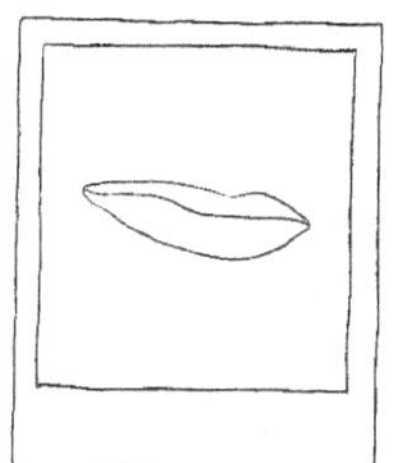

- i just wanna make you smile

there is always a mom
on nights out drinking
i was mom that night
the most sober
the most in control
you & her
were nearly gone
incoherent
we stumble into the uber
i keep looking back at you two
laughing, drunkenly falling all over each other
i feel the pit
in my stomach
this feels off
i look back again
i see your lips meet hers
i die inside
that was so easy for you
so effortless
from this moment on
things will never be the same

- broken

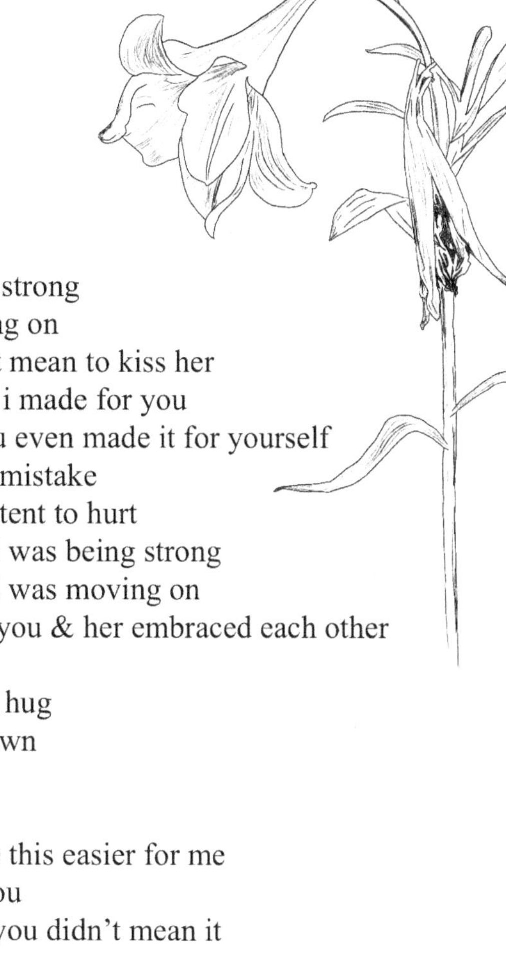

i'm being strong
i'm moving on
you didn't mean to kiss her
an excuse i made for you
before you even made it for yourself
an honest mistake
with no intent to hurt
i thought i was being strong
i thought i was moving on
but when you & her embraced each other
again
in a warm hug
i broke down
hurt
betrayal
help make this easier for me
i beg of you
show me you didn't mean it
please?

i'm being strong
i'm moving on
you didn't mean to hurt me again
by carelessly hugging her
like i wasn't even there
an excuse i made for you
before you even made it for yourself
an honest mistake
with no intent to hurt
i thought i was being strong
i thought i was moving on
but then you did it again
like i wasn't even there
again
hurt
betrayal
again
do you even care about my feelings?
welcome to the darkest night of my life

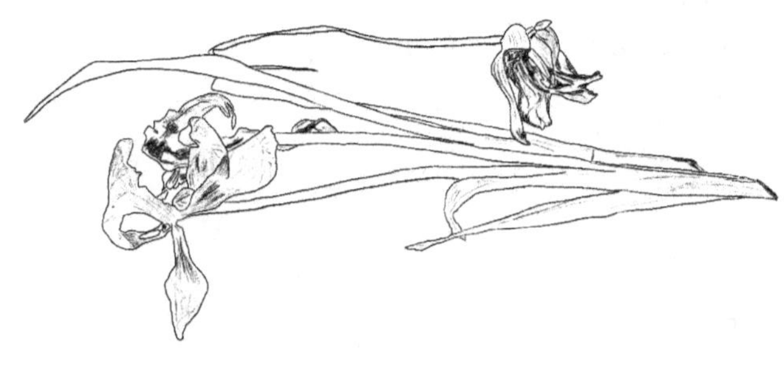

i have tunnel vision
i can't see anyone
or anything around me
rage
anger
pain
overcome me
there is only one thing i know of
that will release this emotion
i run home
i get there faster than i ever have
and go straight for the box cutter
and there i sit
on the kitchen floor
my arms are a blank canvas
ready to be mutilated
so i
slice
slice
slice

the rich, red blood
dripping down my arms
onto the floor
how beautiful it is
and oh how good it feels
the release
so i cut deeper
i push harder
the blood gushes
once i run out of room
i switch to the other arm
and then the leg
i need to stop
painting myself red
before i take it too far
i don't want to die
i just want to feel better
help me
help me
help me

over the years
the weight grew heavier
our love that was once
light
airy
& free
now puts strain
on my shoulders
on my back
although this weight
continues to increase
i become stronger
i become more tolerant
i am willing to carry the weight
no matter how heavy it becomes

- unconditional

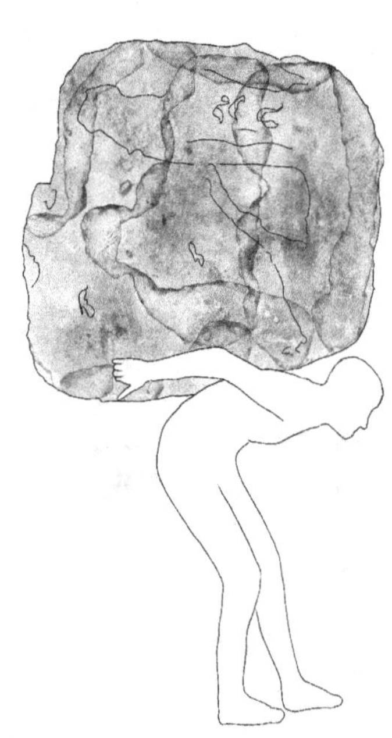

i know you think of yourself
as someone who doesn't cheat
can't cheat
not even if you tried
it's a safe delusion
i hope someday
you can look reality in the eye
and you can come
to terms with it
accept defeat
learn from it
grow from it
and maybe
just maybe
loosen the ridged mindset
once a cheater
always a cheater, yeah?

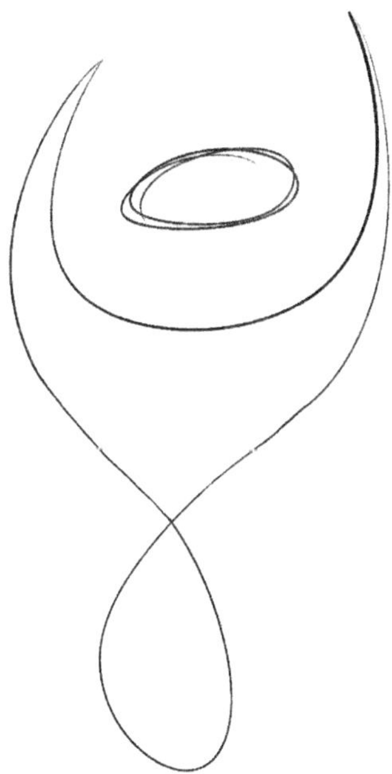

the body is amazing
the body is smart
it tells you when something
isn't right
isn't balanced
when extreme emotional distress
causes your hair
to fall out
in chunks
it's easy to blame
hormones
maybe it's my thyroid
maybe it's this
maybe it's that
but never
maybe its him

- red strands

one day i made the choice
i made the choice
to choose you
everyday
no matter what
to fight for us
for you and me
because i never wanted to live a life
without you
this choice meant many sacrifices
of my own
this meant settling for less
this meant accepting that you may never change
you may never grow
but none of this mattered enough
i didn't care
you were my priority
while i was becoming less of one
to you

i need to hear you say it
say that we are over
say that you are
breaking up with me
because if you don't say it
it isn't real yet
please
just hit me with it
if i don't hear you say it
my heart will think
that you didn't mean
for me to leave
it was all just a misunderstanding
and i'll be back over
for dinner tomorrow
say it
say it
say it
even though it kills me
just give us
a humane death

- denial

that moment before waking
ah, such a moment of bliss
of peace
before the mind
has any time
to even remember
it's own name
who i am
where i am
what day it is
what is happening today
what happened yesterday
dread
it hits
it starts in your stomach
and travels into your chest
as your mind
quickly remembers
your reality
this is when
i remember you're gone
you're not mine anymore
and i am not yours
and it wasn't
just a bad dream
it's like having your heart broken
all over again
every morning

- temporary amnesia

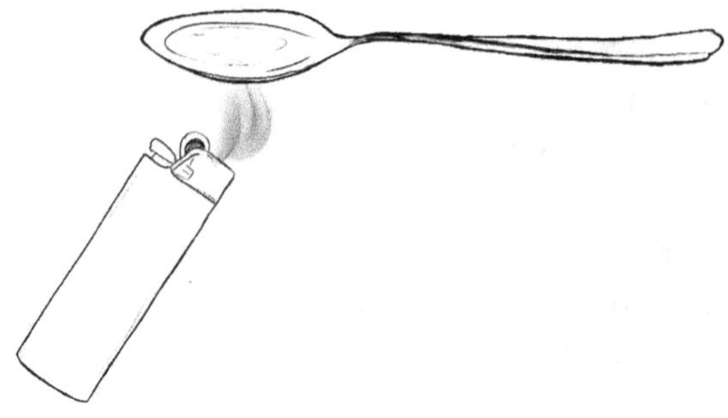

you are my drug
my greatest addiction
always craving just one more hit of you
knowing well that the withdrawals tomorrow
will be unbearable
you're like heroin
and i'm a recovering addict
8 days clean
and not a minute goes by
without you entering my mind
again
again
again

- set me free

we loved each other
no doubt
but did we even like each other?
the number of times
my character was attacked
put down
made to feel
less than
why?
was i that horrible
in your eyes?

reminders
they linger
in the oddest spots
funtown splashtown
claw machines
arcades
my kinda lover by billy squire
flex seal
six flags
shake the frost by tyler childers
friendly's ice cream
rock island line by johnny cash
applebee's
the boys are back in town by thin lizzy
taco bell
i think you should leave by tim robbins
drake
the dried rose petals on my window sill
that i threw away today
i will probably
have five more to add
by the end of the day

you said
that you always wanted me in your life
i believed you
i still do in a way
but you can't pick & choose
which parts of me
you want
i am whole
it's all or nothing

a fading memory
your face fades over time
the little intricacies
the way your eyes wrinkle
in the corners
when you smile
i can't see them anymore
they have become blurry
your voice, it fades
i could replay
your contagious laugh
over & over again
but now it is getting
harder to hear
harder to make out
each little sound
i try harder
to see
to hear
to feel
until it only fades

i will move on
i will heal
i already am
& i will let go
as best i can
but there will always be
that one thin string
attaching us
maybe it can be cut
i just haven't found
the right scissors yet

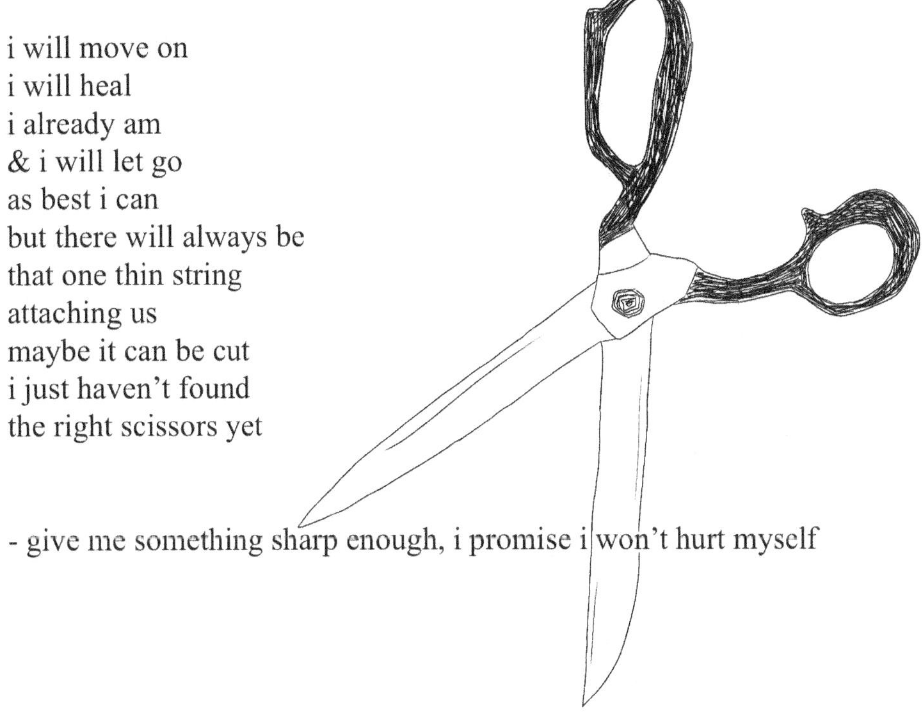

- give me something sharp enough, i promise i won't hurt myself

you taught me things
without even knowing it
you taught me forgiveness
one of my greatest weaknesses
not through example
but through circumstance
your actions
inflicted deep emotional wounds
and i wanted you more
i wanted us more
than hatred
resentment
& revenge
i was left with no choice
but to proceed with
love
compassion
& understanding
i loved you
unconditionally
even when i shouldn't have
i tried so hard for you
but you made it harder
i'm still practicing
forgiveness

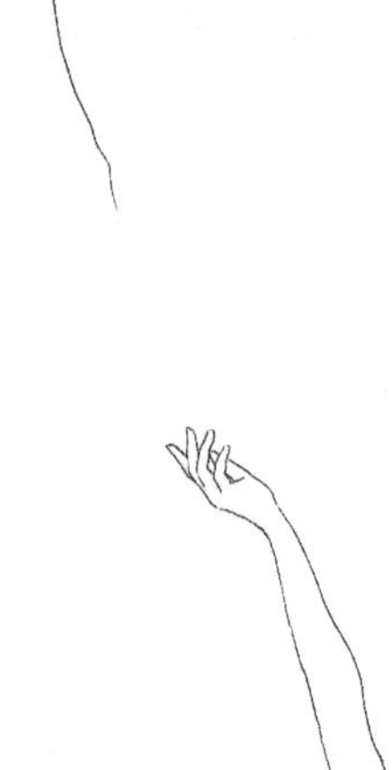

we couldn't swing it
this time around
too much hurt
too much damage
too much pain
all in the name
of growth
we will be okay
no
better, actually
apart
in this lifetime
can a soul tie be broken?
i don't know
but if it can't be
come home to me
not in this body
not in this mind
come in your own time
i know yours will take
much longer than mine
but when the time is right
come home to me

Note From The Author


 A few years ago, I learned from a psychic that I had "a dark stormy energy around [me]" and that I needed to turn to my creativity for salvation. I didn't think much of this until recently when I decided to look inward and discovered that I process tough emotions through my creative flow energy. Reflecting on my life, this makes so much sense. The times I have felt the most at ease, the most free, the most authentic, and the most alive is when I am in this creative flow state. It really is a "state." It's like you go to a different place in your mind, whether through painting, drawing, music, dancing, or writing. The psychic was right, it saved me. And it took me a whole 25 years to fully acknowledge this finding. Now, I prioritize my creativity on a regular basis which has led to the production of works like this one.


Comments, questions, or feedback?
Contact me!


email: lilylamkin1@gmail.com
instagram: lily_lamkin

* 9 7 9 8 2 1 8 0 7 9 0 6 2 *